Songs o

A.S. Newby

Songs of Oak and Ash © 2023 A.S. Newby

All rights reserved.

No part of this publication may be reproduced, stored in a retrieval system, or transmitted, in any form or by any means, electronic, mechanical, photocopying, recording or otherwise, without the prior written permission of the presenters.

A.S. Newby asserts the moral right to be identified as author of this work.

Presentation by *BookLeaf Publishing*

Web: www.bookleafpub.com

E-mail: info@bookleafpub.com

ISBN: 9789357696746

First edition 2023

DEDICATION

For my dear family.

PREFACE

To enter Bookleaf Publishing's 'TheWriteAngle' poetry challenge in 2022, I'm composing this book. The fantasy genre as a whole, as well as myth, legend, fairy tales, and nature, have all served as inspiration. To convey the idea that these tales have always been found in nature has been my goal; the idea that all I have done is listen to what the Earth has to say. It was J.R.R. Tolkien's The Hobbit, which I read as a child (at least I was more of a child then than I am now), that sparked my interest in the fantasy genre and was a big inspiration for this book. It was not all perfect and smooth going; I have encountered some difficulties along the way. Capturing emotion and thought is not simple, nor is it easy. Although it can be challenging, I believe that every writer will eventually find a way to juggle writing, personal life, and education or work. Although it isn't stress-free, I firmly believe that everyone on this earth is capable of achieving their goals if they work to the best of their ability.

Mountains

He skipped and he waltzed,
Through the unyielding flame,
It flickered and it flashed,
Faster, faster he galloped,
While the embers leaped and frolicked around him.

Unharmed, through the blaze went he,
To see these mountains,
In set of three,
Piercing the sky, where the white mist did fly.

Over the forest green and the lakes cold,
Sheltering towns small and towers bold.

He Who Came to Be King

Away went he, when he went away,
Through shimmering night, through glorious day,
Along the path and over the hill,
Under great mountains, wanders he still.

On handsome thrones, in handsome halls,
Still he hears the mountains' calls,
Away went he when he went away,
Through glorious night, through shimmering day.

Over and under his trail has led,
In fields he slumbered, with grass as his bed,
When he went away, away went he,
Over long lakes and under long trees.

Away went he, when he went away,
When he went away, away went he,
Oh, he went away!

Glæd

The water sat, still as can be,
The leaves drifted down, free, and free,
The toads sat upon their stools,
And lily pads upon their pools,
The blossoms burgeoned from the tree,
The rabbits hopped, all full of glee,
The fish ambled in their schools,
And the spiders wound their webben spools.

Pebbles lay about the pond
Strewn or in shapes familiar and fond,
A certain magic was in the air,
The scent of pines was fresh and fair.

In an open door, deep in the wood,
An owl slept as soundly as it could,
For there was not much noise,
And there was plenty of shade.

And all was calm in the ever-green glade.

A Tale of Tails

First there glistened an eye,
When came it closer - a face,
Then a body, then a paw,
And another, and two more.

Sweeping its tail and darting around,
Though looking intensely no mice could be found.

It weaved and wandered through tall mushrooms,
Purple and glowing,
Some bending, some bowing.

It leaped to, then perched upon a cap,
A firefly flew past with a buzz and a zap,
And thus a chase began,
With nothing but its claws,
And a hurriedly devised plan.

Jumping on a tree stump to complete its task,
The fiery fiend was finally in its grasp.

See

To look, to see,
To walk, to be,
To search, to find,
In body, in mind.

A bird would perch upon a tree top,
Absurd to observe and old deer hop,
Odd to the norm, odd to its form,
Odd to its form, odd to the norm.

Such a sight be hard to see,
Shackled by eternity,
Fixed in time,
Fixed in state,
Not a moment too soon,
Not a moment too late.

A toad would sit upon a shroom top,
Observe the absurd clouds drop,
Odd to its form, odd to the norm,
Odd to the norm, odd to its form.

In body, in mind,
To search, to find,
To walk, to be,
To look, to see.

Petrichor

A raindrop hit the watered ground,
With the smell of petrichor in the air,
All heard the deafening ripping sound,
As the heavens began to tear.

A flash of light,
A burst of heat,
Birds startled to flight,
As their wings did beat.

The smell of rain replaced now,
By the scent of singed oak bough,
Fire of wrath, fire that reigns,
Trees burned down to their watery veins.

You need not look far,
You need not look hard,
To witness the effects,
Of the sky's discard.

Observe this now fallen tree,
Gaze at the sky's majesty.

A Dark Night

She sat on a small stump,
In the moonlight, under bat flight,
It was once a great trunk,
In the starlight, on a dark night.

Though whimsical were the trees,
And frenzical - the flowers,
She sat in unease,
Feeling worse by the hours.

When at last she stood,
In awe-full revelation,
She looked, as she should,
As the sun filled its vocation.

She felt, again, at ease,
She realised the notion,
That while cold, peaceful is the breeze,
While cold, water - nature's potion.

Starlight

When the sun sank and the light went on its way,
The night crept down as all looked on in dismay.

Laying on a mossy stone,
Gazing at the bluish dome,
Why must all good things end?
Why must all fabric rend?

Yet, as the night went steadily on,
The moon and the stars brightly shone,
And quiet, like a blanket fell,
There was no ringing nor a bell.

After all, no good things did end,
After all, the fabric will mend,
Although the night is not the day,
The moon and the stars keep darkness at bay.

The War for Ant Hill

From green to orange the leaves have gone,
Thick coats of fur the foxes now don,
On the ground lay acorns, hatted and brown,
And the bugs' moss streets bustled in their town.

The beetles went along their way,
And worms wriggled to their earthen homes,
Spiders' webs of fabric did not fray,
Snails slithered into their spiralled domes.

Once all in the town had shut window and door,
The ants on the hill prepared for war,
Atop a kingdom made from mud,
Raising her sword the ant queen stood,
As the spiders marched their octuple legs,
The guards bow down and the spider king begs.

"Please my lady, spare us this peril!"

"I would not grant peace to one so feeble and feral!"

And with that, the war began,
The ants chased,
And the spiders ran.

To and Fro

The blades of grass danced in the breeze,
While the birds sang,
And the trees looked pleased.

Though waving their arms and shaking their leaves,
Their trunks stood still,
And still they would be.

'Till over they fall,
For the mites to eat,
In a wooden hall,
Where they take their seat.

When the feast was done,
And the trunk was hollow,
The tree did run,
And the mites did follow.

Down the hills and over the sand,
There lies the tree,
Far from the land.

Back to the sea,
All waves must go,
But who knows what will be,
Between to and fro.

The Winter Sun

The trees whispered and mumbled,
Words, by humans never said,
No bees bimbled and bumbled,
But, ran foxes in their stead.

The winter sun,
Or soon it will be,
Had nested low,
Just over the sea.

As gentle waves lapped the shore,
The rabbits burrowed,
And the badgers did bore.

Wearisome grew the hedgehogs,
And tiresome grew the dormice,
They rested in their hollow logs,
'Till long passed the full moon thrice.

When the last leaf had touched the ground,
The first snow had become abound,
A cosy bed of frost and folium on the floor,
As the leaves on the trees were no more.

The plants had now no more to say,
Through the longer night and the shorter day.

Whither and Whence

The path on which all walk,
At least hitherto all have,
Grows wider at points,
And narrower at others.

It winds in and out of the shade of trees,
It forks and it joins other paths and trails,
Merrily singing their balladries,
They walk, sharing their songs and tales.

From odes of joy to records of dread,
Words of courage and wisdom, none went unsaid.

Every now and then past water they wandered,
By lakes, and rivers, and tarns they sat and pondered.

"Whither do we go, and whence have we come?"
Though knowing not their way, lost were none.

Would this journey have no end?
Had it yet even its beginning?
Will it reach its final bend?
Is there way of losing or winning?

None of this could any foresee,
Not the past or the future, only to be.

Freyrviðr

The only sound the birds,
The only sense the gentle breeze,
Close - a fire crackled peacefully,
Far - waves came softly ashore.

Serene was the forest,
As golden sunbeams filtered through the trees,
Serene was the forest,
As the crickets chirped,
Serene was the forest,
As the leaves fell.

Freyrviðr was the forest yclept,
Trees of ash and oak grew their roots in the ground,
Of honey smelt the flowers,
Grass-of-Parnassus their name.

Bliss and Bleak

A war be waged,
'Twixt bliss and bleak,
Upon the sky it's staged,
Not meagre nor meek.

While the light draws its sword
And the dark bares its teeth,
Plays a dissonant chord,
O'er the misty heath.

And the battle would rage,
Upon a sea of clouds,
As the book turns its page,
To the fog that cloaks and shrouds.

Through the haze,
Filtered the sun's bright spears,
Long were the days,
Ere the darkness nears.

Heed

For all and none,
For what's lost and won,
To Earth's gardens tend,
To the heavens' ears send.

Deliver thy message,
To hall and home,
Deliver thy message,
To king upon throne.

May all pay heed!

Sfal's Ward

I have journeyed through frost, through flame,
High above mountains I've soared,
Deep below dungeons, through caves I have wandered.

All to reach this relic.

For something so small to hold such power,
In wrong hands all things it could devour.

I have journeyed through ice, through fire,
Hastily through trees I've swung,
Met beast, while fearsome they roared,
All to find this relic,
All to find this great treasure hoard.

'Tis without chests of gold, this hoard,
Without goblets o' silver, and nary a sword,
Contained within lies only one thing,
For here rests Sfal's Ward.

Red

Come with me,
To where the water runs red,
Come and see,
Where the land lies dead.

Where fire, in the sky, resides,
And where darkness no longer hides.

Here the mountains spew fire,
And the ground births flame,
Death dwells in the spire,
In the air lives pain.

Ere memory, ere light,
Long festered evil's might.

'Till when the sun came,
And the light was born,
Much to their distain,
The shadows lost their form.

Come with me,
To where all are nocturnal,
Come and see,
Where darkness - eternal.

The River Runs

Through great halls the river runs,
In hoards of gold it trickles,
Under and over stone in the tons,
Above valleys of splendour it ripples.

Through great cities the river runs,
Past towering mountains bold,
In tunnels where all light darkness shuns,
Through icy glaciers cold.

Ere at last the river meets its end,
Goes it now straight through humble towns,
Never a turn and seldom a bend,
After its journey, its ups and downs,
By the sea it's at its end.
It's ventured past great Kings, with great crowns,
But by the sea it's at its end.

Vigil

It watches,
It seeks,
'Round all corners it peaks,
An orb in the sky,
Ycleped The Eye.

No one does know,
Why it appeared long ago,
Just know they,
That all things it judges,
All fate it decides.

Beware the vigil of the unsleeping eye.

I ran, and I ran,
Past bodies lying motionless,
Past houses now ash,
Alas, distance makes no difference,
As I run, no matter how fast.

I have heard talk of a sanctuary,
Barricaded by steel,
Safe from all vile watch.

To there I must head,
Leaving nothing in my stead.

Malicious is The Eye,
That is the embodiment of hatred,
That is fear incarnate,
That is the epitome of turpitude.

"Refuge or prison?"
Is what crosses my mind,
I am free, held captive in this cage,
That renders The Great One blind.

Bean Sí

Hark! Hear my call,
Lament! 'Fore the fall.

Under the moonlight,
To you I speak my augury,
Under the stars bright,
To you I tell my tale.

What waits 'round the corner,
Need not instil surprise,
Soon to be a mourner,
Soon red will be your eyes.

Hark! 'Fore the fall,
Lament! Hear my call.

And On

It twisted and danced,
As it wandered through the trees,
It leaped and it pranced,
As the sun fell to its knees.

When the sun returned, still there it frolicked, it waltzed,
'Till soon came thunder in cracks, and lightning in bolts.

Ere the first charge struck it sprinted and it whirled,
Again through the trees it rushed and it curled.

And on this did go, and on, and on,
When at last the clouds cleared,
Revealing no sun,
When at last the clouds cleared,
And the light was done.

Still, it waited and it sat,
And on this did go, and on, and on,
For the light had now perished,
And the sun was gone, gone and gone,
And on this did go, and on, and on.